I0033712

Staying Afloat in the Bathtub Business

© Copyright 2004, Updated in 2009, Andrea Scott. All rights reserved. This book, or parts thereof, may not be reproduced in any form without permission from the publisher.

Published by
Andrea Scott
A SCOTT REFINISHING
720 Oakton
Evanston, IL 60202
e-mail: andiscott@gmail.com
Visit our web-site: www.Evanstontubs.com
ISBN: 978-0-615-26182-9

The opinions expressed in this book are solely those of the author, based on her own experiences. The information put forth is not to be construed as "advice" or a recommendation that will work well in every situation. In no way does she intend for this manual to replace a formal training program. Nor should it be suggested that every refinisher will evolve in the same manner. Geographic location, different training programs, and individual personalities are likely to influence perceptions and choices.

Copyright © 2009 Andrea Scott
All rights reserved.

ISBN: 0-615-26182-5
ISBN-13: 9780615261829

To order additional copies, please contact us.
BookSurge
www.booksurge.com
1-866-308-6235
orders@booksurge.com

Staying Afloat in the Bathtub Business

How to Break Into and Succeed in the Refinishing Industry

www.evanstontubs.com

Andrea Scott

A SCOTT REFINISHING

2009

CONTENTS

INTRODUCTION

My husband was right. I had no business getting into this business. I am not handy. In the fifteen years we have been together, he has seen me tackle exactly one home improvement project. On this occasion I went over the top of the old paint job in our stairwell. I also have trouble operating simple pieces of equipment. He has watched me do battle (and lose) to an office stapler, which is to say I am not good with mechanical devices, like spray guns. When I first told him I was considering sinking money into training for the refinishing business, he laughed. When I told him I was serious, we had a HUGE argument. Of course, the woman always wins or I am quite sure I would not be doing this.

Three years later I am writing this manual. I can say it has all been worth it. Success, however, came with some persistence, and, I sheepishly admit, a bit of help from him.

I wrote the manual to address three different audiences. First, there are those of you who are contemplating getting into this business. I believe the chapters will give you a better idea of what the landscape looks like out there. You'll get a handle on whether it is for you. Secondly, I wrote for those who are new to the business. I am sharing with you most of the experiences I've had over the last three years. I sincerely hope some of what I've learned proves helpful to you. Lastly, if you are a veteran of this business, I hope you can gather some tips from this book. My marketing tips may be especially useful.

My husband may have been correct in telling me I was not a "natural" for this line of work. However, I don't think he understood why I might be well-suited for it. For me, the refinishing business offers several advantages. The job gives me flexible hours and the opportunity to be my own boss. Having a somewhat creative nature, I like working with my hands and putting forth an aesthetically pleasing product. I enjoy the fact this is a high growth industry and should remain so. It is also a career with favorable earning potential.

When I first started in this business I attended two different training programs, presented by two different suppliers. Both were excellent. However, when I started doing the work I realized there was no substitute for on-the-job training. Training sessions cannot prepare you for the real world. They don't teach things like how to know who your customers are, how to deal with their expectations or what kind of work exists out there. I guess the bad news is this manual will not substitute for a formal training program or on-the-job training, either. However, as I evolved I realized much of what I learned would be worth passing along.

It would be totally neglectful of me not to mention the help I got from other refinishers. When I began I had several questions. Since I do not own a franchise I found it necessary to create my own help network. I have spoken with many refinishers on the phone. Without exception, all were generous with their time. I can only speculate as to why so many were so willing to help. This, as I stated, is a growth industry. Few refinishers seem threatened by competition and therefore most are willing to share information. Perhaps they feel they have more to gain by sharing. The more homeowners know about quality results, the more likely we all are to benefit. Whatever the reason, I am grateful for their help. I have always said the least I could do is pass along the favor. I hope writing this book somewhat fulfills this intention. I am sharing with you everything I know, and much of what I learned came from them.

There's another part to my story. I am a writer and performer. This is what I like to spend half of my time doing. The refinishing business offers me the time and flexibility to pursue these passions. If you have other hobbies or interests beyond work, or any of what I have told you about myself describes you, it's likely you're a candidate for this line of work. Hey, if your goal is to spend half your time trying to make it to the big leagues as a Hollywood film producer, I'll sell you the movie rights to this book! (Okay, so it's not Sea Biscuit).

I have also met a few corporate expatriates who are happy doing this type of work. I know of one chiropractor and two accounting types who operate successful businesses and are happy to call themselves refinishers. The one thing we who do the work all seem to have in common is the fact we choose not to work for anyone other than ourselves. Anyway, happy reading. Hopefully, someday I will be hearing from you. Refinishers, as I have said, like to talk about their work. It is always enjoyable to have a conversation with another refinisher.

Chapter 1
DEFINING THE BUSINESS

What is Refinishing Work?

In the beginning, I too had an old dulled out vintage bathtub. I had heard about refinishing but I didn't know much about it. I thought I might consider having my tub resurfaced. Coincidentally, about this time I was seeking a new business opportunity. I needed a job that paid better than the one I had.

For me, working for somebody else (I mean an employer) was out of the question. I went to the bookstore and picked up two books, "Jobs on a Shoestring" and "Survivor Jobs," the latter a book for people like actors and musicians who need second jobs. Since I didn't want to pour a great deal of money into a new business, the shoestring book appealed to me. However, it was the survivor one that listed refinishing as a career possibility.

I became curious about the refinishing business. I went home to the internet and used the search engine to research the industry. I found a training facility five miles from my home. I thought I'd found my calling, or one of them at least. I've already mentioned I have several interests.

I still didn't know much about the process. My husband, of course, was the perfect devil's advocate.

"I saw an episode of 'This Old House' where Bob Vila sprays a bathtub and the whole thing peels before the episode even ends," my husband said.

"Bob Vila's not a bathtub refinisher," I said. Besides, have you ever seen the slightest thing go wrong on one of his shows?" My husband backed off.

In my first training program I learned that the work involves the application of a coating using an HVLP gun, the type of gun used to spray automobiles. In fact, most of the technology and products behind spraying tubs is a carryover from the automobile body shop business. This seems to be changing. Nowadays, there are companies out there who develop products specifically for the refinishing industry.

The company I initially trained with is also a supplier of refinishing coatings. They carry an acrylic urethane coating. Logically, their trainees learn to spray this product. It makes tubs look new and has been proven to be quite durable. There are a number of suppliers out there that deliver on products that last quite well. In my area it is standard for refinishers to issue a five year warranty. Though I would recommend asking your supplier to provide test data on product durability, problems with bonding do not often involve the product. More likely, if there are problems they are due to omissions in preparation work. By "omissions" I do not always mean "sloppy" prep work. In chapter four I'm giving you an extenuating circumstance I ran into involving very old tubs that peeled.

When I started doing tubs I learned that refinishing work should not be confused with giving the customer a new bathtub. Most people were very happy with the work. Many actually wanted to maintain the character of what they had. But a few made a silly distinction- they weren't getting a new tub. It turns out there are people who do not have a complete understanding of what we can accomplish as refinishers. One thing we cannot do is turn out a brand new product. When I first started I didn't completely understand what could and could not be achieved, either. Nevertheless, it turns out there are a few instances we should shy away from taking the work. I could write a couple of chapters about dealing with customer expectations. Hey, stick with me, I have written on this topic throughout this manual. As refinishers we work with coatings, engaging ourselves in a process that is different from re-enameling. Porcelain enamel or any finish that is put on a brand new bathtub can only be applied in a manufacturing setting. The finish is baked on in an oven under factory controlled conditions. This all takes place in some form of oven at several thousand degrees. As refinishers, we cannot emulate the process.

The Growth Picture

The growth potential in this industry is staggering. After three years in the business my phone rings steadily. I don't have a huge advertising budget. For starters, most folks have a bathtub. The only possible exceptions to this rule might be those folks we see on the home improvement channel who elect to move to extreme homes. Still, it would seem likely even people who choose to live in a bat cave or a tee-pee must need some place to shower. Somebody must be responsible for their well-being. Bathtubs dull out over time, colored tubs look dated. The same can be said for tiles, countertops, appliances and (yes) cabinets. A complete discussion on the restoration of each of these items might be beyond the scope of this manual. Consider it more of a fundamentals of refinishing. Nevertheless, you begin to see the built in market for refinishing.

Much of the growth picture these days stems from the fact many people are just beginning to understand that refinishing work can be done with very favorable and durable results. Many consumers are still not familiar with the process, but this is changing. You will spend a fair amount of your time enlightening the customer. All of this is an argument for sharing information with other refinishers. There is plenty of work out there and no need to feel you are in competition with someone else. At the same time, the more refinishers spread the good word about the process and encourage others to do good work, the more work we can expect for everyone.

What are My Markets?

There are several markets for refinishers. These include bathtubs (of course), both residentially and commercially. There is also a market for refinishing work in vintage tubs for resale, cabinets, countertops, appliances and backsplashes. Most refinishers seek their niche because they have a personal preference for one market over another. This manual will explore some of the reasons refinishers make the choices they do. In some cases a refinisher may develop his business as an off-shoot of some other business he owns. I.e. a property manager may choose to save money by spraying his own tubs. An interior decorator may decide he or she likes the hands-on work of spraying cabinets.

I know several bathtub resurfacers who perform both residential and commercial work. The latter involves working with new home builders or hotels, either spraying tubs or fixing chips and gouges on porcelain, fiberglass or acrylic. They also repair acrylic shower surrounds and bottoms. In fact, there are folks who have plenty of business just doing repair work. Many of these refinishers rarely do bathtubs.

Most repair jobs are like mini-refinishing jobs. They are just like refinishing a bathtub in miniature, using the same material. Ideally, to do a proper job with fiberglass or acrylic you will want special materials. I myself have done gel-coat, meaning fiberglass repair. Ultimately, I found the gel-coat product too toxic and gave up on doing repairs on anything plastic. You can use your regular products. They just don't work as well.

Within each category you will find further ways to segregate your market. For example, a bathtub refinisher can deal with a high-end clientele and offer a "deluxe package." This might involve such extra services as replacing the drain and overflow and making a return trip to machine buff the tub. He may find he can charge extra for these services. I believe it requires time in the business to enable a refinisher to segregate his market to this degree. There are many ways to operate a refinishing business. Again, this is a manual that looks at the fundamentals of refinishing. I am also primarily limiting my discussion to bathtubs.

While on this discussion, I might mention that some of the franchises offer extra services as part of their normal package. They charge about 30-40% more than the median price in the Chicago market to refinish a bathtub. I'll give you my opinion. I think it's a hard sell to the average consumer. The consumer generally (but of course not always) recognizes that he/she can obtain industry standard work for a median price. (more on franchises under the heading "Should You Buy a Franchise," later in this chapter).

Start-up Costs

One of the more appealing aspects of this business is the fact start-up costs are low. If you already own a truck or van you can get started for a few thousand dollars. Start-up costs include a formal training program, spray equipment and exhaust system, supplies, franchise fees (optional), advertising and liability insurance. The latter two expenses, like death and taxes are permanent.

The cost of training programs varies. Based upon my own experience and surfing the web, they run between $500 and $5000. Prices vary based upon what is included in the package. Some training programs include supplies.

I personally don't endorse any one training program. I have attended two training sessions, both sponsored by suppliers. Naturally there was a tie to using their supplies. Both distributed fine products so I had no problem with this. I would tell you I opted for a second training program because I felt I wanted more than one perspective.

I would also tell you it is my belief there is no such thing as a true "hands-on" training program. "Hands-on" training comes from being in the field. But for starters, I think it is a good idea to ask your potential trainer what he feels are the benefits of his training and products. If applicable, it is a good idea to get them to send you test data on their products as well.

Once you have graduated, there are a number of ways to get on-going support. This can come in the form of tech support lines, franchise meetings, personal networking and a book such as this. I'd like to put a plug in for this manual. Honestly, I think it is the only comprehensive and objective resource guide that will help you better understand what goes on out there before you dive into the water. This will help you before you run into situations you could not have anticipated. It will eliminate some of the trial and error.

Equipment costs and needed supplies for starting out in this line of work are low as well. A spray system that includes a turbine and gun only runs about $1200. An exhaust system (fan) runs about $300-400. Beyond that, there are incidentals. I've included a list in the back of this book. All told, your equipment costs should be under $2500. These days, with Ebay out there you might even find a real deal on equipment. I know a few folks who have had luck with Ebay. A supply kit of materials to get you started should cost a few hundred dollars. I will leave it to your supplier to help you itemize these.

The two companies that I am familiar with that make spray equipment are Graco and Wagner. There are others. I am also not an expert on all forms of spray equipment. These are the most common. If you are truly interested in all options, I would suggest visiting a specialty paint store that sells spray equipment.

If you do not have a truck or van, it will ultimately prove necessary to get one. Sure, I started working out of the trunk of a Honda Accord, but it didn't give me much credibility. Parking down the street from your client so nobody sees what you are driving is not a great option, either. We do have equipment to carry. I settled on a Chevy S-10 with a tonneau (fiberglass) cover, a choice that has made me happy. I wouldn't recommend anything smaller, however. Actually, it is just the right size. I'll make an analogy between the truck and my purse. When it gets too full I know it's time to remove a few items. At that point I know I am carrying stuff that is unnecessary. I am also glad I own a truck. This way the chemicals are in the back where I can take a vacation from them.

My liability insurance costs me about $600 a year. Of course, I have no one working for me. Beyond that, refinishers don't need licenses and we don't pay union dues. This part is nice.

I feel I run my business on a very low advertising budget. Marketing strategies are covered in chapter eight.

Should you Buy a Franchise?

A late brother of mine owned a moving company franchise. He used to complain about having to pay royalties and advertising fees. He didn't feel the ad fees were worth it. I guess this turned me off to the franchise idea.

I do not have a franchise. However, they may not necessarily be a bad idea. One (franchised) refinisher told me his franchise created an essential networking opportunity and was therefore instrumental to his success. Truthfully, I can understand this. I would gladly have paid a tidy sum of money for help when I was starting out.

I think the bigger issue for me, however, would be living by franchise rules. I simply do not want to be limited by territory or products. Most franchises do tell you where to operate and what products to use.

I will share with you a few things I do know. As I stated earlier, a franchise in my area charges about 30-40% percent more to refinish a bathtub than I do. They offer some bells and whistles I don't, such as caulking and machine buffing. This involves a return trip. [Note: It is now 2009. I am charging about $385.00 per bathtub. The franchise charges about $550.00]. I can deliver a good result for my price and make a decent profit. Also as I said earlier, I am merely speculating that the franchise price would be a tough sell. I am not sure it represents the market for this type of work.

Besides, paying more doesn't necessarily guarantee a better job. The three franchisees I am familiar with have a great deal of overhead. They generally need to maintain a stable of technicians. I may as well throw in my two cents about hiring technicians. None of the franchisees I know are particularly successful at training and maintaining technicians. This is a skilled business and it is not always easy to find good workers. Also, remember that we work with chemicals that destroy property. Workers are not always conscientious. Finally, it seems to me the franchises have a difficult time paying their technicians well when there is a great deal of overhead involved.

One particular franchisee in my area has a warehouse/showroom and does quite a bit of expensive advertising. Not long ago, his franchise headquarters placed a full page ad in the Chicago Tribune. Full page ads in the main newspaper of a major market are bound to be expensive. Directly or indirectly this franchisee must be paying for it.

Google Adwords directs enough traffic to my site to bring me enough business (see my marketing section). I probably spend less than $300 a month on them. Darn good I think. It makes me wonder if a franchise is worth it.

I will tell you the approach to training I would have taken, given the opportunity to start over again. It is pretty much the path I did take, though knowing what I know now, I could condense the time frame if I did it again.

I would highly recommend a week long training program. There is a lot to learn. Preferably, it would be one that emphasizes general methods. This, as opposed to spending a great deal of time on how to use a specific manufacturer's product. Subsequently, it would make sense to take a

two and a half day training program with a particular supply house. Choose the product you plan on using and stick
with it. They all have their quirks. It is not likely you will want
to switch products very often, after adjusting to a specific
one.

I once heard from another prospective refinisher. He
wanted to know if it made sense to buy another person's
business. I couldn't see doing this. There is a great deal of
work out there. I am not sure paying for an existing customer
base is worth it. Equipment costs can be quite inexpensive
as well, so I don't know if you need to purchase someone
else's business for their equipment, either. I do know refinishers who have bought their equipment on Ebay.

Chapter 2
WORKING WITH THE CUSTOMER

Who is the Customer?

Most customers are hardworking people like us who respect our efforts and are fun to work for. They don't care if you make a mistake as long as you come back and correct it. Customers generally realize you are not delivering a factory direct product, and frankly most aren't obsessed with having a brand new bathtub. If you like what you do chances are you'll wind up holding your work to a higher standard than they do. Most folks will not get out a phase contrast microscope to view your work, but there are exceptions.

Your work will satisfy most of the people who even think they want to hire you. You should be able to satisfy eighty percent of those out there. Of course, that leaves a critical twenty percent. Here, we are dealing with two kinds of people who are likely to wind up unhappy. The first category involves people who have expectations that are too high regarding what refinishing work can accomplish. They are dealt with in this chapter under the subheading, "When expectations are too high." The second category revolves around people who are difficult and unreasonable for reasons we may never uncover. They are dealt with in this chapter under "Some Customers are More Challenging than Others." Unfortunately, in either case, it is the smallest percentage of customers who will give you most of your problems. Because I know too well the frustration of dealing with a few tough cookies, I'm going to spend time on this topic.

When I was in college I took statistics and learned about the bell curve or "normal distribution." For our purposes the bell curve tells us that if we are exposed to large enough sample of people we can formulate a distribution of their responses to our work. For the sake of argument we will say it is consistently good work. Most customers will tell you they are quite happy with it. However, the bell curve distribution has two ends or tails. On the favorable end of things a few customers will make you feel as if you have changed their lives. There are customers who will tip you, cook for you or send you a card at Christmas. At least, these are all things that have happened to me. Okay, maybe they were just nice folks. But let's just say again for the sake of argument that these are customers I was able to make even happier than most. The other tail comprises the responses of people you will flat out never satisfy. The bell curve, by its mere existence tells they are out there. The reason I use this illustration and make such a big deal out of it is, because, this is the way it is. Once you realize this you will be less inclined to take negative feed-back seriously. Forget it. Some of these people have had miserable lives and they're taking it out on you. Further, I'd like to again make it clear these negative types exist in the minority. However, a small group can make a job unpleasant.

This manual and experience should help you filter out customers you shouldn't be working for. If you can do this, chances are you will have found a career you enjoy. These days I hope that no more than five percent of my customers wind up unhappy. Can I do better than that? I don't know. I'll keep working on it.

When Expectations Are Too High

I chose this business because I am happiest working for myself. I suppose I might even be at my happiest if I didn't have to work for anyone. I don't mean not work period, I mean not have to work for customers. I work very hard targeting the kinds of people I can make happy, screening for those who might be disappointed. For me it simply isn't worth doing work for people you can only disappoint.

There are two kinds of customers who may have expectations that are too high. The first category involves people who do not understand the limitations of your work. The second type of customer, I believe, is an individual who should really be in the market for new fixtures. Let's talk about the former category first. You may be unable to completely smooth out a pitted bottom, alter the texture of a bathtub, or disguise a chip one hundred percent. Or things aren't feasible. Doing the work to truly fix something would require too much of your time. Naturally, you would want to charge for your work. In many cases, this is not what the market will bear. Also, there is also no such thing as a perfect spray job. Skill will always be a factor in this type of work and nobody is that good. Even the best refinishers are likely to leave behind a small amount of dry spray. Of course, this can be buffed out with very fine sandpaper.

In these instances, it is necessary to shift an expectation or you may wind up with an unhappy customer. If there is something you cannot accomplish to perfection, it is best to point out the problem before you do the work. Not only will you learn more about who you are dealing with, you will establish credibility by telling the customer what you can and cannot do in the first place. When you complete the work, they will know you have given them the best work possible.

Of course, there are times when you cannot shift an expectation. It becomes even more imperative that you find this out sooner rather than later. These are jobs you probably don't want to be taking.

14

I would like to share a story that illustrates a couple of points I have made so far. It should show you why you never want to overestimate a customer's expectations. I refinished a standard bathtub for "Mr. Pocked Marked Tub." Let me make it clear I am making a reference to his tub, not his facial characteristics. The rail of his tub was covered with microscopic hairline scratches so numerous the landscape had been altered. The inside was also porous and had a uniformly non-uniform topography. In retrospect I believe this tub had to have spent part of its life outdoors or maybe a machine shop somewhere. It seemed scratched by out-door elements.

I sprayed the tub and the customer was unhappy. He couldn't understand why I couldn't get a smooth glossy sur-face. "The coating will only deliver a smooth finish contin-gent upon the surface underneath," I explained to no avail. I was telling him after the fact.

Subsequently, a refresher course with my current sup-plier revealed there was a way to handle this situation. I could have applied many coats of primer and waited a half hour in between. This would have turned the job into a two day project. Naturally, I would have had to charge him two and a half times as much. Would he have paid it? Frankly, I doubt it. As I have said, the market isn't there for this level of work. This customer was fairly irate and I ended up refunding his money. If I had covered any limitations with him up front he would not have had a leg to stand on.

For my money the second category under our heading "When Expectations are Too High," tends to revolve around people who own higher end homes. There are people out there who simply do not know refinishing a tub will not give it a brand new, from the factory, sheen. The sheen will not match up and there may be imperfections. I suppose I could argue that Mr. Pocked Marked's expectations might put him into this grouping, too. When it comes to categorizing tough customers I'm hoping the reader can accept a certain amount of overlap.

At any rate, there are people who do not know they are really in the market for new bathtubs and tiles. It may be your job to tell them. Part of my customer demographic includes potential clients with pricey homes along Chicago's lake shore. Let me tell you about the PINK HOUSE.

Not long ago I went to do an estimate for some tile work at an upper end residence. The homeowner led me down a pink hallway past some pink pictures and up some pink stairs. When we arrived at a pink bathroom she announced, "We're selling and the realtor is objecting to our pink bathroom."

I'm not sure one less pink bathroom would have made a difference. Nevertheless, this wasn't the concern I expressed about doing the work. The tiles and sinks were both contemporary and top of the line quality, suitable for the Kohler showroom, located in Kohler, Wisconsin. The truth is, a refinished bathtub and tiles will not carry quite the same sheen as ones you might see at a Kohler or American Standard display center. This is a case where going over the tiles might have diminished the look of them. This, along with any imperfections in the work, would be even more evident under skylights or in ideal lighting conditions. Many more expensive homes have the latter features as well. The pink house was no exception. I also felt the large surface area would have raised maintenance issues for a future homeowner. There was more area to scratch or chip. I took a pass on the work.

I should point out again there are plenty of people out there who are not in the market for a showroom look. Some of us, in fact, have vintage homes. We prefer a look that is more in keeping with the character of what we have. There is a plenty big enough market for people who want refinishing work.

16

"Mrs. Perfect" was another potential client who lived on the north shore. This was a job I didn't take either. "The work has to be 'perfect,'" her decorator told me. I'm not sure if "Mrs. Perfect," had a voice in her own home renovation. She didn't seem to want to deal with the common folk, and I'm not sure she wanted a home that a commoner might occupy, either. I had a hunch she would only be happy with brand new bathtubs and sinks and I told her so. Be wary of customers who tell you they want perfect work.

Then there was Mr. and Mrs. Micro. I should have known something was up when Mr. Micro first phoned me. He asked a lot of questions and kept me on the phone for a half hour. I have since come to the conclusion a phone conversation about a bathtub shouldn't last more than five minutes. I shouldn't have been surprised when he turned out to be just a bit too analytical of the work.

After I finished Mr. Micro's job I received a call-back. When I returned there were stick 'ems all over the bathtub. Mrs. Micro was down on her knees with a utility lamp. Were Mr. and Mrs. Micro people who didn't understand the limitations of my work, or were they customers who were in the market for a new bathtub? Or were they just plain difficult to deal with? I'd say all of the above. I don't think it matters. I only know they were customers I didn't need.

Some Customers Are More Challenging than Others

Mr. and Mrs. Micro definitely fell conveniently into this category. These people could not be reasoned with. I should also tell you that when I returned Mrs. Micro had masked the entire bathroom, floor to ceiling. She had thrown out the toilet and replaced it because a small amount of overspray had gotten on it. Worse, she didn't want to pay me. In fact, I have yet to receive payment from Mr. and Mrs. Micro. Ultimately, a mechanical lien was placed on their property.

There are also people who, I believe, are hiding something and don't want to communicate with you. Let me tell you about "Mr. Evasive," a building owner who hired me to do several bathtubs. He fell short of paying me for all of them. This is a guy who opened the conversation by telling me the last refinisher he had hired hadn't followed up on his mistakes. Be wary of customers who aren't specific about telling you what they don't like about your work or anybody else's. No doubt there are some bad workers out there, but this guy showed me why someone might not come back.

According to this man the work wasn't satisfactory. Twice we made appointments so he could show me what he didn't like. Twice he didn't show up. At one point he had his son call to tell me the tubs weren't done right. No specifics here, either. At least I cut my losses early and didn't start new work when Mr. Evasive started to make me suspicious of his character. Even so, in the end I didn't get all my money. The moral of the story is two-fold. Never do work for anyone who isn't direct with you. Secondly, never let anyone get too far ahead of you without paying.

Sometimes I think a job that falls through is a mixed blessing. Most of us would rather find out sooner than later about work that is going to give us problems. Not long ago I showed up at a customer's two-flat with the understanding that I was to spray two bathtubs. I was met at the door by my contact's wife. She informed me that he was still sleeping and that she didn't know I was coming. Further, they were attending a funeral that day. It wasn't going to be a good day to do the work she informed me.

I thought about that one later. I always look back on jobs that fall through, specifically so I can learn from them. In this case, I had noticed this property was rather run-down. Six hundred dollars would have seemed a large chunk of the owner's budget. I have encountered potential customers who became silent when you give them your prices over the phone. This man was one of them. It seems those who are most embarrassed to admit they can't afford the work will often put up a smokescreen. It is easier for them simply not to show up. With all due respect for departed souls I don't think this man's wife leveled with me.

My husband, my beloved editor, calls this manual "navigational." If you have not been involved in the business very long it will help you navigate through uncharted waters. If you have a bad experience with one customer you may able to generalize about others a great deal sooner. I can't always tell somebody what customers they should be dealing with. Sometimes knowing how to judge people comes with experience. However, when you meet a tough customer you can always come back to this manual. Soon you will recognize that some of the customers you come across will fall under a pattern. Hopefully, the manual will help you pick this up sooner. This means you will spend less time dealing with the wrong people. Hopefully, it will also help you get over a bad situation more quickly. You'll understand that some customers are just plain difficult to work for. This has nothing to do with you.

People Who Don't Pay You

Rarely, I have worked for people who didn't pay me. In retrospect, I don't believe these folks had any intention of paying me in the first place. In the long run I didn't find them rational. I've had people tell me I broke something I didn't or that they've seen refinished tubs before and they looked a whole lot better than the ones I just did. I let it pass and learned from it.

Sometimes you will encounter potential customers who have come recently from other countries. They've lived with evolving economies. They were not always exposed to an economic system as nice as ours, and may seem a bit overwhelmed by it. Be compassionate, but also be careful when doing business with them.

I have friends who are contractors and subcontractors. They tell me some of the games people play so as not to have to pay you are as old as the hills. Never take this kind of treatment personally.

The only recourse in these situations is to put a mechanical lien on their building. This involves going to the Recorder of Deeds office in your city and getting a legal description of the property. Forms for filing liens are available at office supply stores. Unfortunately, customers who don't pay people do have a lot of tricks up their sleeve, and this process has yet to yield me any money. Mr. Evasive's name wasn't listed on the title to his own alleged property. A phone call to the proper owner yielded the reason. Mr. Evasive owed him money, too, for the contract sale of his property. The proper owner hadn't transferred the title because of it.

I encountered another situation where a customer did not want to pay me. I went to the court house a couple of times. The file was perpetually missing. I don't think this was by accident.

I could make this an even better book for the kind of customers who are looking for ideas, but sorry, I'm not going there. Putting a lien on a property fulfills the principle of the thing. Fortunately, this sort of thing does not happen very often. I'd put my payment default percentage around 1.5%.

Experience should allow you to virtually weed out customers who don't pay. In 2008 I did not have any non-paying customers.

Setting the Tempo

I don't think I could overestimate how much I have learned about the need to control my own time. Never give your time away unless you want to become the Salvation Army. With a bit of planning it isn't difficult to get things under control. Every customer is looking to get the most for their money. I don't suppose I am any different. We as refinishers cannot expect the customer to acknowledge our side of the business. He or she may not understand how costly it becomes for us to make extra stops or return trips. Obviously, return trips mean you are making less money an hour on the job. I have also learned that placing a high value on your time leads the customer to place a higher value on your services.

I have learned never to give my services away for nothing. My competitors charge to come back and caulk or replace shower doors. I usually send someone else who charges. The following is a composite of several phone conversations I've had with callers. It illustrates how things can go wrong when you let customers take control of your time. Okay, I've heightened things a little. That's what I like to do.

Ring..Ring...
Me: A Scott Refinishing.
Customer: Oh, hi. How much do you charge for a standard bathtub?
Me: We charge $385.00.
Customer: And do you come back and caulk for that, too?
Me: Well, not normally. Our competitors charge to do that. But I guess we could, as a favor to you.
Customer: What about shower doors. Do you mind taking them down and coming back to put them back up?
Me: Yeah, okay. You're right in the neighborhood.
Customer: I need you to pick up the keys as well.
Me: What's the address?

I suppose I should have simply offered to pick up a case of soda pop and swing by with a pizza. A bad situation can get worse. Let's take the guy who wanted the caulking job done. He informed me when I arrived at his place he'd found somebody else to do it. When that deal fell through he called me at eleven o'clock Thursday night, demanding that I show up and do it before the weekend.

After all, I'd said I would. The woman who wanted me to pick up the keys sent me to an address on a crowded college campus. There were "no parking" signs everywhere and a parking ticket was $125.00. Foolishly, I took a chance. The keys didn't work in the building anyway. Refinishing is inherently fun and challenging way to make a living. Don't let customers turn it into something different.

I have a couple of strategies I use to avoid a return trip. I have noticed that some of my customers, particularly the ones in higher-end neighborhoods, are not the most price sensitive of my clients. They demand greater service but rarely complain about having to pay a bit more for it. For them I quote my prices a little bit higher. Why not? I know they are likely to ask for frills anyway. I may as well cover myself for it.

When I have a phone conversation with a potential customer who asks about extra services and return trips I know it may not be enough to tell them over the phone that I charge for these. Sometimes they will pressure me when I arrive to do the job. I tell them over the phone it's "company policy" not to return for any service. Then I send them a price list ahead of time.

Once in awhile a customer will ask me to give him a reminder call the night before. I tell the customer I don't normally do this because I'm afraid I'll forget. I have made a note to call before, however, when people inform me they are having the tile work done in their bathroom first. Contractors are notoriously behind schedule. Often they don't call until the last minute to tell you this. I always check in ahead of time if I think there is going to be a problem. I don't want to be the one inconvenienced.

Things to Know Ahead of Time

There are a few things we refinishers require to do the work. These include running water, heat and electricity. The customer doesn't necessarily know this. You can avoid making return trips by asking a few key questions over the phone. Ask the customer if the plumbing is a new installation or if the house has been vacant. If it has, the water and heat may have been turned off and you need to find this out. If you work in a cold climate it is always important to find out if there is heat in the building. Apartments and rehab projects do not always take place in buildings with heat. Cold rooms mean your coatings will flash off more slowly and runs are more likely. A tub that takes longer to dry costs you time and allows dust to settle, dulling your finish. The coating may not gloss over as well either. Ask the customer to turn the heat up if possible.

I get another question from potential customers who are rehabbing their bathrooms. They want to know at what point they should have their tub refinished. I tell them that I will come in at the very end. Otherwise, there will be too much debris in the room. Working with drywall behind you usually doesn't work too well. Ultimately, this will end up on the tub. This usually necessitates a return trip for the refinisher. He/she will have to smooth out the bottom and often respray it. It is always a good idea to wipe down the wall tile for dust prior to refinishing a bathtub.

Clawfoot tubs also present a set of challenges. Ask the customer where the tub is located. Many are kept in basements or garages, which can be dusty. Make sure there is no debris coming off the ceiling. A clawfoot should never be sprayed in an area with a pilot light from a stove or furnace. I have sprayed a few without running water by running a hose, or if the tub wasn't real dirty, by using a bucket of waster. Garages can be cold as well. Make sure the environment is the way you need it to be or be prepared to make adjustments.

You can read more about fixing clawfoot tubs in chapter four, under the heading "Different Fixtures."

Chapter 3
PRICING

Setting Your Price

In 2009, bathtub refinishers around the country are charging anywhere between $100 to $600.00 to resurface a standard bathtub. Pricing varies highly by market. San Francisco is perhaps the highest market in the country. In the Chicago area a reputable refinisher wants between $350-400. The franchises generally want more. Across the country I have talked to refinishers in Columbus, Dallas, San Antonio and Ventura, California and Albany, New York to name a few. In Illinois I have spoken with refinishers in Chicago, Wheeling, Joliet, Waukegan and Palatine. The latter four communities are outlying areas. Good, experienced refinishers from these parts fall into the $350-400.00 price range. If you live in a market smaller than Chicago you might have to adjust your price down from this.

The best way to find out what people are charging is to simply call around. If you make ten calls you will begin to find a consensus. Some might call this the median price range. There will likely be some refinishers who fall below this median range. I wouldn't worry about these individual too much. There is always someone out there willing to undercut a price. Most likely he or she is cutting corners somewhere, but it is unlikely you will be able to prove this. Even consumers realize this. Okay, not all of them. However, as long as you are competitive you should be able to get your price. Commercially speaking, refinishers do come down on prices to accommodate work in apartments or hotels. This is because the work can be done in volume and the work is easier. Property managers of apartment buildings usually are often not as fussy about the work as well.

Holding to Your Price

I am a firm believer if you are quoting a competitive price you should be able to stick to it. In the beginning I took what work was available and occasionally came down on my prices. I came away with an observation. The customers who balk at a fair price are usually the hardest to deal with and often hand you some of the more difficult work. As a matter of fact, the very few times I haven't gotten paid (for good work) involved customers who haggled on my price. Kind of begs the question doesn't it? If they didn't plan on paying me why did they try to get my price down in the first place? These days when I get a customer on the phone who doesn't like my price it sends up a red flag.

Here's just a little more strictly personal commentary: I generally just don't get involved with bidding situations. Granted, I don't take many big jobs since I really don't have any employees. Nevertheless, I consider most of them more challenging than they are worth. Contractors and project managers with the tightest budgets will also usually manage to hand you the most difficult type of work and situations. For my money, single family dwellings with no walk-ups are nice places to work. Pink tubs waiting to become white are even better. They are usually in pretty good condition.

Add-Ons

Add-ons are a nice way to make extra money. Selling them is a good habit to get into. They generally come with a good mark-up. In fact, I think selling add-ons is essential. They will help pay for material costs, thereby driving down your expenses. The three most popular add-ons being sold are skid-resistant surfaces, drain covers and cleaners. A skid resistant surface can be applied between coats so that you don't have to make a return trip. Sometimes the customer is looking for a cosmetic fix for an ugly drain. There are trim kits available that can be glued on over the old drain. These are popular with customers who are selling property. My supplier also markets a consumer cleaner. Initially, I wasn't big on pushing it. Most customers thought they could do better at the store. Eventually, those who did purchase it gave me an endorsement by calling to order more. Turns out it is economical and works about the best of anything. These days I try to sell more of it.

Chapter 4
SHOULD YOU TAKE THE WORK?

Old Stuff vs. New

I think I have a fun job. Nevertheless, I am a woman who works alone. I don't employ anyone. My other half helps me occasionally. I am much happier taking the type of jobs that are manageable for me. I would like to share some thoughts on how I pick and choose my work. For one, I live in a community where the homes are very, very old, with many landmark homes that date back to the turn of the last century. A great number were built in the 1920s. I have seen some very old stuff. It has its challenges and I do not choose to do this type of work exclusively. This factor has even provoked me to target my marketing more toward communities that seem to have more post-World War II development. This is a business with many dimensions and there is lots of work out there. All refinishers find their niche. For me, the condition of the work is a factor.

I'll share one story with you. The other day I went to do an estimate on a vintage tub a few blocks from my house. It was a clawfoot variety with a flat bottom. The tub was a dinosaur with paint cracking off the sides. The faucet was dripping. Judging from the amount of corrosion around the drain, it perhaps had been dripping since 1917. Nostalgia would be the only reason for keeping it.

I knew I could easily get in over my head if I tried to do the work. I worry about underbidding jobs. Of course, if you have a handle on what needs to be done you can charge extra for it. However, this may not be what the market will bear. In this case the customer insisted "he only wanted it white," but this is a situation where it becomes very difficult to second guess a customer's expectations. Painting it white would simply have exposed more of the flaws, something he may not have anticipated. This is the domino effect as we say. I took a pass on this one.

In the beginning I suppose I felt guilty for not taking work if I wasn't very busy. I have since learned it is important never to need the work that bad. I want people to be happy with my work. In my opinion this sometimes involves being selective about what you types of work you accept in first place.

Sometimes folks who are moving will call and ask you to perform down and dirty tasks just to clean things up a little bit. They may not even care if you warranty your work. Examples of these jobs may include the aforementioned clawfoot or going over tiles that are peeling in several places. I think it's only human nature to go in, not know what you are getting yourself into and wind up spending extra time on this sort of thing. Pretty soon you've underbid the job. If you care about your work you may never make yourself happy. I'd advise not doing the work if you're afraid the end result may not be something to which you want to attach your name.

Different Fixtures

There are jobs that I took when I started that I wouldn't take now. Customer expectations and avoiding jobs that will give you difficulty are only a part of it. It can also be said certain types of fixtures refurbish better than others. As I've always said, it is perhaps best not to have customers who are disappointed. Below are some thoughts on spraying different types of fixtures.

Vintage bathtubs—It is unlikely you will run into as many of these as I do but they are fun. Frankly, I have run into a fair number that don't need to be refinished on the inside. They often clean up nicely. I try to be honest with folks because I know they appreciate it. In the end, I feel this is what being in business is a about.

The oldest tub I have ever done was in a coach house not far from my house. It was built in 1830 and literally a few doors down from a place where Abe Lincoln once slept. If you like old stuff you'd love working in my neighborhood. I'll even give you some of my stripping jobs!

Most often, when a customer calls to have a clawfoot refurbished there are a few steps that can be taken. The outside of most antique tubs are roughed up and peeling. These tubs need to be sandblasted. Some sandblasters are mobile, though generally they request that the tub be in a garage or an unfinished room. Of course, a tub can be taken to a sandblaster. You might save a bit of money. However, these fixtures are heavy and it is probably not worth the cost savings. Once the outside is sandblasted it needs to be repainted rather quickly or the tub may rust. Sandblast the OUTSIDE of the tub only. I did have one customer sandblast the inside. It ruined it.

If you are feeling charitable you can tell the customer he can repaint the outside himself. Rustoleum makes a product for doing this. It is an aerosol. Or, have them ask a specialty paint store for some advice. A satin finish often looks more authentic, less painted than a sprayed on high gloss.

I usually charge a bit less to spray simply the inside that I do for a standard bathtub. However, clawfoots come in three sizes, so adjust accordingly. If I spray the whole thing, figure about a third more. High gloss over the whole thing looks fine. Satin on the outside looks better.

I suppose the proper order for doing this would be 1) sandblast the outside 2) spray the inside, then 3) spray the outside and cover any overspray from having sprayed the inside.

Tiles—I don't spray as many tiles as I do bathtubs. This is because they hold up better than bathtubs. Call me conservative on this matter. My husband doesn't agree with me on this one, but what do men know about decorating. I'll give you my take on this matter anyway. I think resurfacing brings the sheen of tile that's in good shape down a notch. It can even remove some of the character of a room in an older home (again, my opinion). I live in an historic area. I have gotten calls from people who wanted to change their tiles. I will many times talk them out of it. They have tile work you cannot find in other parts of the country, or buy anywhere. A good decorator can work with it. Also, remember to remind the homeowner or contractor about repairs. Any grout work needs to be done before you show up. Refinishing changes the color. It does not make up for flaws in the original surface.

Sometimes people are unhappy with the color of their tiles because it can date a room, say back to the 40s. Here, too I also believe in spraying the tub white and finding a good decorator to work with the rest of the room. Of course, again this is just me. Bathrooms carry a number of features that can be changed. Luckily, there is plenty of work out there. I don't worry about talking myself out of a job. I think old tiles provide an opportunity to be creative. However, if tiles carry an old and dull look I see every reason to spray them. I do take my fair share of them.

Also, you might ask your tech support line about using semi-gloss coating on cermanic walls instead of high gloss. I have discovered it looks less "painted" on. This applies to matte finish fiberglass surrounds as well.

Very occasionally, I do get some other calls regarding tiles done previously that are beginning to peel. This is a bad set-up and one I personally choose not to deal with. Most refinishers I know do not strip wall tiles. Some of my competitors do and I am actually quite happy to turn the work over to them. I simply prefer not to be stuck in a room with that much aircraft stripper, even with protection. Also, stripper tends to get in the grout lines and is difficult to remove. Of course, I cannot verify whether my competitors are stripping wall tiles chemically. They may be simply sanding them down and charging the customer a stripping fee. Either way, this is more work than I am interested in doing.

Once I received a call from somebody trying to sell a home that had some peeling tile work. They asked if I could patch up a few places. This doesn't seem to work. Where a few tiles peeling there will be others that will continue to come apart as you work. Color matching would be another issue.

Jacuzzis—A dulled out Jacuzzi can be sprayed with great results. Here are a couple of considerations, however: Most of us are not using a product that will endure around spray jets. These cannot be warranted. Water pressure in this area erodes the finish. I also have a prejudice regarding spraying Jacuzzis in very good condition. I feel the refinisher and customer need to consider a trade off in terms of maintenance on a large hot tub. This is the argument I put up on page 17, when I brought up the pink house story. If you do spray them, use the air hose of your spray system to move water from behind the jets beforehand; remove fittings and spray them separately.

Sinks – Bathroom sinks can be sprayed with good results. But here are a couple of things to think about: They do take wear and tear. Most refinishers are not warranting nicks. Most sinks are in well-lit areas. Imperfections in resurfacing work will be more obvious. If a drop-in sink is in pristine condition but the wrong color I usually try to convince the customer to live with it. A blue sink is an accent piece, not necessarily an unfavorable one if the right color choices are assembled around it. A blue bathtub, on the other hand, may be a blue elephant sitting in the room, a good reason to change it.

I do NOT recommend doing kitchen sinks at all. I once did one. The homeowner called me a week later, because it had discolored. I went back and used my prep cleaner to get it clean again. She called me a few days later, on Christmas Eve. "The sink is brown again," she said. I asked my supplier his policy on kitchen sinks. He told me he'd quit doing them years before. People throw substances in kitchen sinks they don't in bathtubs. Metal utensils nick and scratch kitchen sinks. After too many call backs he quit doing them. Some refinishers do them and don't warrant them. In this book, jobs that come back to haunt you aren't worth it.

Shower bases—Shower bases can be sprayed like anything else. Once in a while I get a call for a Terrazo shower base. These bases are made up of small stonework with filler holding the pieces together. Sometimes the filler disintegrates and leaves roughs spots in between. These are tough to fill. It's also difficult to guarantee an even look all over. They may take extra coats of paint as well. Another comment on terrazzo shower bases: sometimes they have some kind of waxy filler that rests on top. You must etch or clean them very, very thoroughly.

Shower doors- I usually ask the homeowner to bring the doors down before I get there. Most of them involve a guide that can be removed by taking the screws out. Bring the doors down off the track and mask the track, which does not have to be removed. I have found a few tricky shower doors. I generally ask that the customer at least verify that the guide comes off and they can be easily removed.

Appliances—Frankly, I don't do these. There isn't any good reason I don't do them, it's simply that I get very few calls for appliances. I tend to only work with economies of scale.

A CAUTIONARY NOTE ON MOVING STUFF

Never move old stuff. It is not a good idea to move any stuff. Never let a customer talk you into removing a fixture you are not familiar with. Call the plumber. I once moved a clawfoot about a quarter of an inch and it created a leak on the floor below. To wit, this particular customer also wanted me to remove a faucet fixture to spray behind it. This is a plumbing issue as well. Refinishers are best advised to avoid doing these things.

A CAUTIONARY NOTE ON TUB AND TILE JOBS

Follow a system when spraying a bathtub and wall tile. As refinishers we get calls for a standard tub and tile job. This involves the tub and a three wall surround. The tile must be sprayed first, before the tub. This is because the spray gun must be kept the same distance from the wall while you are spraying. Otherwise you run the risk of getting an uneven finish, dry spray alternating with a gloss. The only way I know to do this is to stand on the tub and maintain an easy reach. While spraying tiles, cover the bathtub with a pre-cut cardboard piece to keep overspray off the bottom of the tub. Overspray from doing the tiles will come off the wall and land on the tub. You will need to wipe down the tub thoroughly before spraying it.

While I am on the subject, be careful anytime you are spraying work that is not within easy reach. Not long ago, for the first time, I encountered one of those square tubs. I thought I could reach and decided to spray it the same way I would a standard tub. I couldn't reach the back and finished with many drips. A tub of this nature needs to be sprayed in halves, back, then front. I should know better.

I have another comment on spraying tiles. Generally, I find I need to pick a swatch and change direction on every pass. I.e. spray the first pass horizontally, the second, diagonally, the third, diagonally the opposite direction and so forth. Otherwise, the walls will sometimes look streaked. With my current product, I finalize the job by spraying with clear reducer about six inches away. It gets rid of auras.

A Few Other Considerations

I tend to stay away from requests that I feel are obscure. A few of these that come to mind are barber sinks, acrylic tubs that have been done before and again, appliances. I am concerned that I will underbid the type of work I am not used to doing. I simply tend to avoid variation if I can help it. This is something you may want to think about if you are just starting out. As a general rule, if I can't picture an object from the customer's description I avoid it. If I felt I was writing this manual to give advice, one of the strongest pieces I have to offer is this: You can cherry pick your work and still have a successful business. This is something I never heard from anyone when I was starting out. I do believe I could have saved myself some aggravation.

I live in a close suburb of Chicago. I tend to either avoid jobs in the city or charge extra. I have noticed that most customers inside the city limits will tolerate my "city charge." After all, I'm dealing with traffic, parking problems and some of the high rise condo rules are just plain ridiculous.

I also believe there are times you may want to turn down work because it is the right thing to do. The other day I showed up at a very large and very old home in Evanston. This home had a plaque near the front door stating it had won an architectural award in 1931. I had been called to spray an original tub. When I started working the tub cleaned up beautifully. Because of the nostalgia this area evokes I felt I would be defiling historic property if I resurfaced it. The customer was extremely thrilled with the result. He thanked me and assured me he would pass my name along. I did not charge him the full price for refinishing work, only a cleaning charge. I lost a little money by doing the right thing but the gratitude of the customer made it worth it.

Colors

Ninety percent five percent of my customers want white bathtubs. A few want bone (half white, half almond mixed), almond or biscuit. I carry these on the truck and don't charge extra for them. These are neutrals. I seldom – almost never – get requests for colors. It is a sign of the trends. Consequently, I don't do them. Handling colors is time con-suming and, by my way of thinking, simply not worth it. I always tell the customers who do want colors that part of standing behind your work is standing behind the look of it. I tell them darker colors don't look as good or maintain as well, which is true. If these arguments don't work I try asking the potential customer if they plan on selling their home anytime in the near future. If they are, they should be aware they may turn off a potential buyer. I get calls almost weekly from people who want colored tubs sprayed white, never the other way around. If somebody insists on having a color, I normally pass on the work. I feel if my logic up to this point hasn't appealed to these types, they may be irra-tional or even a little eccentric. These are two good reasons not to do the work in the first place. Mostly, I tell them I care about my work and consider it my duty to help them make the best decision.

A CAUTIONARY NOTE ON ROTATING COLORS

Rotate colors in storage to save product. I do some-times carry black or dark colors for spraying the outside of clawfoot tubs. I live in the clawfoot capitol of the world. If you do carry colors darker than bone or almond it is a good idea to rotate the containers by turning them upside down every couple of months. This moves the pigment around.

Chapter 5
DOING THE WORK

What are the Steps?

I would like to simply present an overview of the steps involved in refinishing a bathtub. There are excellent training programs available. It would be quite difficult for me to imagine anyone embarking on this business without participating in an on-site training program. Naturally, you would be given information about the process. I must also make it clear I am not a chemist and have not tried or tested every product out there. This chapter will not amount to an exhaustive discussion on the types of products available.

As I stated earlier I myself have attended two very good training programs. Based on these I will share common information on what to do. The steps are as follows:

1) All silicone caulking must be removed. Silicone simply will not mix with paint. Silicone is the stuff that is rubbery and will pull up in long rubbery strips. If you are not sure what you are dealing with try applying some coating on top of it. If the coating creates fish-eye you are dealing with silicone. Fish-eye is a descriptive term. The coating will bubble or otherwise not stick to the silicone. I happen to use a product that will not fish-eye, but it doesn't stick to the silicone. Many types of caulk can be painted over. Even caulk that is a hybrid, meaning it contains some silicone content, can be considered paintable. Most refinishers in my region do not remove the drain. We mask around it. The one refinisher I know in my area who does this offers a deluxe package for a high end customer base.

He replaces the drain and overflow and charges for this. I remove the overflow. Generally I do not have problems with this. The customer replaces it later. One time I did break some old screws while removing an overflow. It is best to back off from anything that is not easily removed. Don't remove anything ceramic, either. It might break. It is acceptable protocol to tape off a drain.

2) The tub is thoroughly cleaned with a one or two step cleaning process. All soap scum must be removed, with a blade if necessary. Soap scum is like black ice. You may not always see it very well, but if it's there it can come back to haunt you. Most beginners will experience at least one problem with this. If you are spraying a tub that has been done before it is especially difficult to remove, the old coating will absorb it. If you are spraying a tub with a soap dish, count on seeing soap scum below it. Soap scum can be anywhere. In all likelihood there will be a column of it under the dish. The front walls of the tub also commonly attract soap scum, but it can be anywhere. I haven't met any cleaners that remove soap scum completely. I always wind up using a blade or sandpaper. There are three things that won't mix with your coating. They are: water, soap scum and silicone. It is also a good idea to wipe down walls with a wet sponge for dust control. Dust is the bane of any refinisher's existence.

3) Either an acid etch or a wipe-on bonding agent are used. Etch is used on porcelain surfaces or pressed steel tubs with an enamel finish. Likewise, bonding agent. Bonding agent will not harm other surfaces, it is simply not necessary. Etch will rough the surface and make it more porous. This, of course, promotes bonding of your primer.

A chemical bonding agent promotes bonding as well. Some suppliers are fond of telling you a bonding agent will not work. [Note: It is now 2009. I have used a bonding agent with great success for 7 years now. It works].

4) If etch is used, all residue much be thoroughly rinsed off. (Test with a blade to make sure you gotten it all). A solvent such as lacquer thinner or acetone is then used to remove any remaining etch. If a bonding agent is used, the solvent would be used beforehand.

5) Fill any chips with automotive body putty. Feather sand completely.

6) Use the hose to remove water on the top edge of tub and around the drain. Tubs will peel around the drain if they are not dried properly.

7) Completely mask area to be sprayed to prevent overspray. Cover horizontal surfaces with drop cloths.

8) Use primer (either spray or wipe-on) per the instructions you have been given.

9) Spray topcoat per instructions.

A CAUTIONARY NOTE ON SPRAYING

Spray differently with different types of material. I have sprayed with acrylic urethanes and an iso-free ep-acrylic, in that order. I currently use the ep-acrylic. With the acrylic urethane I had trouble getting rid of roughness, even after I had used it for several months and felt I should be close to being up to speed with it. The ep-acrylic dries very quickly coming out of the gun and you risk dry spray by spraying too far away with it. I spray 4-6 inches away from the surface. I had a harder time spraying after I switched materials than I would have had if I'd started from scratch. When I moved to the ep-acrylic I also initially experienced pooling and runs. I found I couldn't be so heavy handed with the material.

The runs were eliminated by not overlapping more than an inch. You may be able to do a decent job of spraying a tub within the first ten to twenty attempts. Nevertheless, both products I've used had their quirks. The fiftieth job you do will look more professional than the tenth.

A CAUTIONARY NOTE ON OLD TUBS

Be more cautious with older bathtubs. I spray many of the vintage twenties deep caste iron tubs. When I first started I had a problem with peeling on these. Most came several months after I had done them. I consulted with a couple knowledgeable refinishers who pointed out to that old tubs are very, very porous. The old porcelain is like a sponge. Therefore, moisture becomes a problem. Drying times between steps is critical. One suggested I give these tubs a very heavy solvent bath and wait thirty minutes so it would be good and dry. These days, this is my standard procedure. It seems to have helped.

A CAUTIONARY NOTE ON WEATHER CONDITIONS

Be aware weather conditions can affect your material. I seem to have the most problem with runs when the weather is both cool and damp. This necessitates cutting back on the material flow and really watching the overlap of spray.

While on the subject, I'll give you what I know about cold weather and chemicals. Cold temperatures will not harm your coatings or solvents. It can affect cleaning materials, so never leave cleaners in the trunk of your vehicle in freezing weather. This will render them ineffective.

A CAUTIONARY NOTE ON FIXING RUNS

Modify the big gun for use as an airbrush gun to avoid blistering from underneath. Runs must be dealt with carefully. Use this technique if you are returning to repair a run or rough spot. Simply turn the material flow knob to half the level you would want if you were spraying the entire tub. On my Graco gun I give the knob one turn from the tightened position. Normally, I spray full tubs with the material flow know turned about two and a half times. Adjust the fan to a circular configuration. Spray six to eight inches from the surface to avoid any "popping" from underneath. If you need to get rid of any "aura" or line spray clear reducer over the top. To do this, open the material flow knob one and a half turns.

Since I am on the subject of airbrush guns let me mention I must have four types at my disposal. I already mentioned the first. I also carry the Pre-Val disposable variety. They are easier to carry, cost about $6.50 a unit and can be reused if you clean them carefully. For areas that are not critical they do the job. You won't have to carry heavy equipment. I have an airbrush gun I paid about forty bucks for that I don't use much anymore. For chip repair I have upgraded to a much higher end airbrush gun that produces a much more refined result.

Stripping

Personally, I think this is the most important heading in this book. This information would have saved me a couple years of my time. Stripping bathtubs is extremely physically challenging. I'm going to cut to the chase. For the most part, I don't chemically strip tubs.

If you bought a transmission shop and were new to the business, customers would start giving you work. Over time you would come to realize that some jobs are more profitable than others. I have found it difficult to make my money stripping bathtubs. I know I am not the only one who feels this way. Another refinisher in Ohio tells me he simply prices himself out when it comes to stripping bathtubs.

Okay, I might chemically strip a bathtub if the customer tells me he used a do-it-yourself kit. That is the one time you might be guaranteed an easy stripping job. These kits do tend to generate work for seasoned refinishers.

In the beginning I was told by two different veterans of the business that the task of chemically stripping a tub takes about an hour and a half. The product commonly used to remove an old finish is called aircraft stripper. It is lethal stuff that burns your skin and will make you high and very ill, if you are exposed to it while not wearing a mask. An organic mask seems to work far better than nothing but is not an OSHA approved filtering device. I found I could strip a tub chemically in an hour and a half or less in fifteen percent of all cases. The rest of the time it took me much longer. Or, I couldn't remove the old product at all.

I learned that my competitors were charging merely $85.00 to strip bathtubs. With labor and supplies I simply couldn't understand how they did this so cheaply. Since then, I have learned there are shortcuts. Still, my philosophy regarding stripping has not changed. I just tell customers I am a woman working by myself. The work is too challenging. This is absolutely true. I would not be able to remain in this business if I had to strip too many bathtubs. I'll say it again. I turn away a lot of work.

There is plenty of work out there. Sure, some of these peeling tubs might not be too bad. But I can't always tell over the phone. I generally give them to someone else. Most refinishers seem to take the work. I can only tell you what I know about the process. You can then decide whether it's for you or not.

Technically speaking, stripping does involve the use of a chemical to remove a previously applied coating that has begun to lift or peel. All aircraft strippers contain methylene chloride. The product is sold under different names. Most of the refinishers I spoke with had varying degrees of success with different brand names of stripper that listed methylene chloride on the back. The most effective products stay wet longer. Also, it is necessary to work in a warm room. I do understand there are some organic forms of stripper out there that are less toxic. I haven't really worked with them. You'll have a hard time convincing me that stripping, whatever product you do use, is worth doing.

Most refinishers I've spoken with have good success with aircraft stripper. All will tell you they run into the occasional tub that can't be chemically stripped. At least it can't be stripped in a reasonable time frame. Let's define a reasonable time frame as between forty five minutes to an hour and a half. Stripper should cause the surface to bubble up within five to ten minutes. When it's working, the job may sound like an egg frying. If you test several spots and the old surface does not bubble up within a few minutes, you have a good bond. The tub many not be strippable. It is possible to simply feather sand any chips and, if necessary, use a polyester, bondo type filler on them. After using filler you can simply spray over the old surface. One recommendation for stripping a tough job chemically that nevertheless does need to be stripped is to put tin foil down over the stripper and leave it overnight.

There is way to get information on how well the previous job has bonded. If you have a bond, you simply do not need to strip it. Ask the customer how long that old surface has been on there. A job that has been on there for over seven years and has not come up in many places has bonded quite will. There may even be occasions where you run into customers who do not realize their tub has been done. If you are new to the business you may have a hard time telling as well. Grab some wet/dry sandpaper and sand a bit in an inconspicuous spot. If the tub has been sprayed the sandpaper will yield some coating and the paper will turn the color of the tub. I have learned from experience to be more wary of situations that involve peeling rather than chips. Spots that peel are those that tend to keep going at least a few inches when you place a blade under them.

If the tub was sprayed a decade ago and it's holding up with just a couple of minor chips or nicks, you're are probably safe going over it. If there is just one spot that is peeling that's okay, too. I just go over the top of the old surface. If I am not completely sure what I was dealing with I will use stripper to test the tub in several spots. However, I have found many tubs in my area where the overall bond is spotty. In places it comes up easily, in other spots it can be difficult. In any case, if I am not sure what I am dealing with I refer it to another refinisher who will be physically able to chemically strip or sand it. Stripping can be hard work. I said that

It is also common to find tubs that are peeling simply around the drain. A lot of folks don't realize that a leaky faucet or recessed area where water pooled will pull up the finish. I wouldn't hesitate to feather down the area around the drain and go over the whole thing. Always advise the customer you cannot warrant for leaky faucets or pooling water.

Removing caulk from a tub that has been done before will pull up the old caulk. I tell the customer I can try to feather the edge. However, if it is too difficult to feather, i.e. the old stuff is too hard, they may have to simply caulk over it.

I have already mentioned that I have never had much luck stripping tubs chemically. This may be owing to the fact that everything in my area is old and sometimes has been applied in layers. I also know that one prominent refinisher in my area applies a product that is impervious to methylene chloride. They have been in business for about thirty years. I encounter a great deal of their work. However, after about a decade or so their product will begin to chip, just like anyone else's. I can recognize the look of it and I have never seen it actually peel. The product they use is very hard and difficult to feather sand. These tubs are a lot of work and I try to avoid them.

The refinishers I have talked to will take different approaches to stripping. One, in a market not to far from here says he rarely chemically strips a tub. He sands down the old stuff and goes over it. This individual compared a tub that was peeling to wallpaper. "Just because one place on the wall is peeling doesn't mean the rest of it is," he says. Occasionally, this refinisher will strip to the waterline. I have also heard from folks who will strip the inside but never strip the outside of a bathtub. "When was the last time you saw the outside of a tub peel," this one asked me. True, it happens rarely.

Even the two people I trained with held differences of opinion on what needed to be stripped. The first of two trainers is located in my market. He generally strips the old surface. However, if a finish had been on for awhile and was coming up in a couple of spots, he would chip fill and shoot over the old stuff. My second trainer was adamant about removing the old finish every time. I'll say this. I would find it nearly impossible to adopt this policy in my market. He says he is especially wary of warranting the work of a predecessor. The bottom line is whether the refinisher has a strong degree of confidence that his work will hold up atop of someone else's. I personally think it takes time to get a handle on this. When in doubt, bow out. It's easier (and more economical) to turn up your google ads to draw more business. See my discussion on google ads in my marketing chapter. It's definitely out there.

I have sprayed over a couple of tubs that did come back to haunt me by peeling. In retrospect, these are not tubs I would spray over now. In both cases my memory serves me that they were spotty or somehow uneven in appearance in the first place. Also, about one in three tubs in my area has been done before and is peeling or chipping significantly. Even if the work weren't so difficult this is too many tubs for me to want to strip. Of course this decision cuts into my referral business. Nevertheless, I am able to work around it. I have expanded my commercial repair business and am working on my web-site so I can get more business. There is more than one way to make a living at this business.

If this whole discussion on stripping seems rather scary, it does to me too. Just know that you can avoid having to do it. Find someone else who wants your referrals if you don't feel like stripping tubs.

A CAUTIONARY NOTE ON STRIPPING

Apply stripper properly for best results. Use a china brush. It works best when applied by using the brush in one direction, overlapping slightly. Applying stripper over top of stripper deactivates it. **CAUTION: NEVER EVER STRIP AN ACRYLIC OR FIBERGLASS TUB!! THIS WILL DESTROY THE BATHTUB.**

Buffing and Polishing

A bathtub can be buffed out after it has cured using a machine polisher. Or you can do this by hand using a 2000 sandpaper and a polishing product like Finesse, purchased at an auto paint store. This is something a few refinishers do, although obviously you must make a return trip and therefore charge for it. I personally do not do this. Most refinishers I talked to do not return to buff tubs. I don't think in most areas the market exists for this. Folks aren't willing to pay for it.

Cleaning and Maintaining the Bathtub

Customers have many questions regarding what they should use to clean their bathtubs. The bottom line is this: abrasive cleansers (including Sof-Scrub) and bleach products should not be used on a bathtub, whether it has been refinished or not. Mildew dissolving products that can drip on the tubs are out as well. My supplier sells a product that is quite effective, and pound for pound it is fairly economical.

A popular product available from Home Depot and Walgreen's is Simple Green. It will not harm refinished bathtubs. Fantastic and 409 are safe but they don't always do a great job and can leave a ring. Products like Scrubbing Bubbles do a good job but they do contain bleach. If the customer does choose to use the latter it should be rinsed off immediately.

Mistakes I've Made (So you may not have to)

Chemistry never was my best subject. It never held any real fascination for me. Perhaps it's because I never received a chemistry kit for Christmas. These days I am in awe of the fact I work with chemicals that can completely destroy one substance and do absolutely nothing to another. I'm not going to pretend that working with chemicals is my favorite part of the job. They do raise unique challenges and can ruin other people's property. After a while, working with them becomes somewhat second nature. However, one should never become too nonchalant about using chemicals. It is always possible to make mistakes. I would like to run down a list of the chemicals we use refinishers use and share some mistakes I made as a beginner. Again, I hope this saves you from repeating them.

Stripper—Stripper destroys vinyl and lacquer covered wood floors. Both floor types exist out there in bathrooms. Obviously wood floors are much rarer than tile floors. When you run across a wood floor, it is wise not to strip the outside of the tub. You won't be able to avoid hitting the floor. Also, early on in this business when I was re-spraying a tub that had been done before, I neglected to notice that the walls had been sprayed previously as well. I ended up with stripper on the wall. Naturally, it removed the old coating. It was a classic case of fixing one thing and destroying something else. We've all heard from customers about workmen who are guilty of doing this.

48

Solvents—Solvents will destroy lacquered wood floors and marble floors. If you do spill a bit of paint, never use solvent to try and remove it. It will take the floor with it. Have extreme respect for wood floors. Once I was carrying a plastics bag of used paint materials over a wood floor. It burst and got paint on the floor. Henceforth, I always double my bags.

Etch—Etch destroys any baked on enamel surface. This goes for wall and floor tiles. Once, again early on I was doing a tub and wound up with etch on my sock. It was a job I was doing at a discount so I could get my business up and running. While I was doing the tub my sock left a nice dull mark on the shiny floor tile. Later the customer told me she was really planning on gutting the bathroom soon anyway. I've always relished my role as facilitator, helping people make their decisions.

Coatings—Honestly, I am too paranoid to ever spill an entire can of paint on somebody's wood floor or carpet. However, once a gallon of gloss white spilled in my truck. It got on the bottom of some containers, some clothes and on the turbine. I didn't realize it. When I brought my equipment in I got paint on the wood floor and spent the next hour scraping it off with my fingernail. My story gets better. The same gallon of paint dripped on the driveway. It came through the hinge of the tailgate. Paint on a porous cement driveway is very difficult to remove. I asked my contacts for a couple of strategies but nothing really worked. An ounce of prevention is worth a pound of cure. It is best to keep coatings in a bin where they can't tip over. It is also the reason I prefer to store my paint in the plastic containers with the safety caps.

I use a product that is sprayed about four inches from the tub. It dries quickly and the overspray only travels about a foot. Nevertheless, I have learned to be exceptionally careful regarding walls that have been painted dark colors. Mask so you don't spray close to them or your coating will appear on this dark surface. Free release tape should be used on painted walls.

Miscellaneous—I have scratched drains when sanding around them with sandpaper. I have dinged a couple walls while moving my equipment in and out. I happen to live in a house where nobody would even notice. This is not always the case with other people's homes. I think it's important to acknowledge the environment you are in.

Warranting Your Work

In my area most refinishers warranty their work for five years. However, I am aware of the fact some refinishers around the country will warranty their work for longer than five years. Warrantees usually cover any peeling or flaking. Nicks are not considered to be under warranty.

It was once suggested to me that a refinisher should perhaps not warranty his/her work for longer than he/she has been in business. I.e. if a refinisher has been in business for only six months they should only be handing out six month warrantees. I found this a bit impractical. I know I would not have been able to compete in my market if I'd adopted this policy and I could never have gotten in the business. However, it is a bit disconcerting for me to think I am warranting work for longer than I have been doing the job. The only way around this, I feel, is to ask your supplier for names of refinishers who have used their system for several years. Talk to the refinishers about the success they have had. It does give peace of mind. I also know refinishers who advocate testing every product you intend to use. I have to admit I find this impractical as well. I work on a lot of old stuff. Sure, I could test the product but it would be difficult to match the conditions I find out in the field.

Of course no resurfacer likes going back to do warranty work. I hope the suggestions throughout this manual will help you avoid some of it. Over time you will become skillful enough to avoid warranty work almost all together.

There may always be a few times when, despite your best work, you still get stuck doing warranty work. You will get a call back from the customer months after completing the work. Every one in a hundred fifty jobs I have problems with unexplainable peeling. Sometimes contaminate is involved and there is no way I could have recognized it. There are, however, reasons you may get call-backs in the beginning. These will involve situations that could have been prevented. They include the following: improper removal of soap scum, not having the area dry around the drain (always use the air hose to move water from this area) not removing silicone or not allowing enough drying time between steps on tubs that are old and porous. These tubs, as I mentioned, tend to soak up moisture like a sponge and require extra drying time.

Chapter 6
YOUR SPRAY SYSTEM

What are the Components?

The spray system refinishers use involves a turbine and a spray gun. Currently, I have a Wagner turbine. I have Graco remote gun and a Wagner gun as a back-up. Both work equally as well. This system is not necessarily a highly complex feat of engineering but there are several things one needs to know about maintaining it. A gun that is not working will stop you in your tracks, complexity of its workings not withstanding. Mostly, I will talk about maintaining the turbine and keeping the gun clean.

A third component to your spray system is an exhaust system. It operates independently of the turbine and gun. A good fan will draw moisture out of the air and move dust out the window.

Maintaining the Turbine and Eliminating Debris on Your Work

Let's start with the turbine. The turbine must always be kept out of the room. There are a couple of solid reasons for this. The first involves safety. There is a very, very small but real chance you might get hurt. The tech rep at the Graco distributorship gave me a story about a refinisher who was beat up pretty bad when a spark from the compressor ignited with the chemicals. While I am on the subject I have heard of a couple of other fires. One involved a cigarette, the other heat gun. Heat guns are not considered by most to be safe tools to deal with.

The other reason to keep the turbine outside the room involves a more common problem. Overspray drawn into the gun will ultimately wind up on your finish if you continue this practice. (Don't ask me how I know this). It can be costly to have your turbine cleaned. Down-time from not working generally proves to be more expensive. I know of no reason to disassemble and clean it, however.

While I am on that subject, there are other reasons particles can wind up on your work. One involves dust in the room. This happens frequently when the tile surround on the tub has been done right before the refinisher arrives. Debris and dust from the walls ends up on the tub. When faced with this situation it is probably a good idea to wipe the walls with a sponge. It is also a good idea to shut windows and vents in the room to prevent dust from blowing. If the floor is dusty carry a spray bottle and spritz the floor. If the turbine is in a dusty area elevate it onto a box. Room dust is something most of us struggle with continually. Between my second and third (final) coats I make a practice of using my hand to remove any debris that has landed in the tub. Especially look for dust if the tub has a wide rail.

A CAUTIONARY NOTE ON DUST IN THE ROOM

Minimize room dust for a smooth finish. Dust in the room is a constant challenge. Debris in the finish diminishes the look and makes customers unhappy. Here is my check-list for minimizing debris (and call-backs!!) Bear in mind you may never totally eliminate either.

- Clean filters on the turbine regularly. Use dish soap and rinse regularly.
- Obviously, the gun needs to be clean.
- Don't prep the tub with water that is hot. Debris lands more readily in a humid room. If you use etch products with too hot of water it can damage mirrors.
- Always rinse down walls, tops of showerheads and tile ledges. Eliminate dust in the surround.

- VERY IMPORTANT. Take your bare palm and wipe down the entire bathtub right before spraying.

The last reason for dust getting on your work involves the canister. Particles can ride through the stem inside and come out through the spray gun. There are strainers available for this. Presently, I seem to be able to get away with not using one. I simply need to make sure there is no debris in the bottom of the canister before I begin working. Consult your trainer on this.

A CAUTIONARY NOTE ON ORANGE PEEL

Maintain a proper mix of material to avoid an "orange peel" look. If you are left with an orange peel effect after spraying, either the ratio of your paint components is off or air flow through the gun is compromised. The latter effectively alters the coating mixture. Either of these conditions can lead to roughness or an orange peel effect. The finish will look like the surface of an orange. I always do a check of the valves and couplings on my gun before I begin working, making sure the valves are open and the couplings are tight. There is nothing more frustrating than making a couple of passes on your tub without realizing the material is grainy. Not all roughness is orange peel. Dry spray and debris can also create roughness.

The advice I have received on fixing roughness has been pretty consistent. Of course, grittiness involves a return trip. If the tub is only slightly rough you can bring down the coarseness by using a fine 400-600 sandpaper and using a Finesse-like polish. Finesse can be purchased at auto paint specialty stores. If it is much worse you can sand it down more aggressively and apply another topcoat. In this case it may be necessary to apply a light coat as a barrier before applying a gloss coat. For my money, it is very difficult to bring down any level of coarseness caused by orange

54

peel. This is why I am so adamant about checking equipment.

Cleaning the Gun

Both guns that I have used were essentially cleaned in the same fashion. At the end of the job the cup is emptied of any material. This material is placed in a can. Later, when you have accumulated enough, dispose of it in an environmentally safe manner. Contact your community sanitation department on this one. The air valve nearest the gun is turned off if necessary and solvent is run through the nozzle. With the Graco gun it is best to use a circular spray configuration as opposed to a six inch fan.

With the Wagner gun I employed this process, but brought the gun home for soaking in a dip bucket. The components (with the packing) sans any plastic parts went into the dip bucket.

I have never soaked the Graco in the dip bucket. It is, however, a good idea to disassemble the nozzle every few days and soak the air cap and non plastic parts. Don't remove the packing or black piece that controls the fan. Use a small amount of petroleum jelly to put the needle back in the gun.

It is always a good idea to talk to the gun distributor about cleaning procedures. The Graco rep suggested I backwash the gun while cleaning it by putting my thumb over the nozzle. He also recommended occasionally removing the needle and inserting it in reverse (from the front) to see if the the nut behind the packing requires tightening. If the needle moves too freely paint can move through there. It is best to tighten it. I have not found a need to do this very often.

If you need your gun professionally cleaned or serviced it is best to send it to the manufacturer or supply house from where you purchased it. Actually, I am able to take mine to a local paint store that is also a Graco distributor. I do this every 2-3 months. This usually works quite well. They once made the innocent mistake of turning a bleeder into a non-bleeder gun. This is a small matter but I didn't realize it worked against the gun configuration I had. It could have led to a backwash of coating into the material hose.

Maintaining the Gun

My Graco gun does require maintenance. The inside of the gun, particularly near the pig-tail needs to be free of paint when you finish. This means it is inadvisable to fill the canister more than three quarters of the way full. I usually stop around 21 ounces. Never tip the can. Keep it level and try to avoid movement that causes sloshing inside. If, at the end of the job, paint is at the top of the canister use a small spray bottle to rinse it down with solvent. It is not a good idea to remove a cup gasket without replacing it with a new one. It is also a good idea to keep solvent in the line between jobs. Make sure the can is clean before using it again.

I'll share a couple of episodes that disabled my gun. The first incident involved putting too much paint in the gun. Paint found its way to the back of the pigtail, cutting air flow. I also left a job with a small amount of paint adhering inside the rim. Later the can and top assembly could not be separated. I have also dropped the nozzle of this remote unit with the machine turned off. This sends paint down toward the air cap.

I feel it is a good idea to own a back-up gun. I have two guns. Every three or four months I send the gun I have been using back to the Graco distributor to get it cleaned. This way I always have one gun to swap out.

The Exhaust System

The exhaust system I have found most effective is a carpet drying fan. It is purchased through an industrial supply company and will put out 300 CFM. We were taught to create a tube using 3 ML plastic and duct tape. The tube goes over the output of the fan. The long tube then is then unfurled and becomes routed out a window with a screen removed. When in use, HVAC filters are placed over the screens to avoid overspray getting into the mechanism. The fan is kept outside the room.

Chapter 7
SAFETY EQUIPMENT

How Bad are the Chemicals, Anyway?

I rarely think about the chemicals anymore. I've found good products and good safety equipment. The products I use these days may be milder, but it is foolish to work without safety equipment. Chemicals can be inspired and absorbed through the skin. Therefore I will start at the top with safety masks.

Masks

There are two kinds of breathing systems, filter mask and fresh air systems. The former involves cartridges that filter out the chemicals. The latter involves air pumped in from another area all together. Generally speaking, the fresh air supply system is more expensive and cumbersome.

The first year I was in the business I used a coating that contains iso-cyanates. At the time I was only using a filter mask. Ten months into the job I began to experience chest pains. This was due to the iso-cyanate acrylic urethane product. This condition was serious for me and I knew I had to fix it. The only true and OSHA approved means of protecting yourself while using an isocyanate product is to use a fresh air supply respirator. I had mixed feelings about switching to a fresh air supply system. I didn't feel I wanted to be inconvenienced by the unit.

About this time I went to my second training seminar and decided to switch to an iso-free product. Ultimately, this is the set-up that worked for me. Several refinishers using the ep-acrylic iso-free product have good success with the 3M 5200 series (filter) masks. They can be purchased at paint specialty stores or Home Depot. I have since learned that there is such a thing as a turbine system that houses a fresh air supply unit. This would certainly cut down on the baggage. I would also not want to suggest that everyone may want to switch to an iso-free product. Some feel an iso-cyanate product has superior hardening ability. Nevertheless, I prefer the look of my product and the durability is quite good. I would still rather not be bothered by a fresh air system. The following is a look at safety as it relates to the various products we are using:

Stripper—The methylene chloride product commonly known as stripper is the most toxic product we are working with. Though odorless, it renders the user nauseous and very light-headed almost instantaneously. Although a filter mask may provide some protection, the only authentic, OSHA approved way to protect oneself is by using a fresh air supply mask. Proper glove protection and some sort of spray suit are also in order.

Solvents—Our exposure to solvents may be limited compared to other materials we are using. Nevertheless solvents such as gun cleaner (otherwise known as lacquer thinner) or acetone are more harmful substances to breathe than the coatings material. Use them with protection.

Etch or Bonding Agent—Both of these products are dangerous for your health. Both require the use of a mask. Etch in particular can burn your skin and is very bad for the eyes. Never use etch without wearing goggles, a long sleeve shirt and gloves.

A CAUTIONARY NOTE ON FILTER MASKS

Take breaks if wearing a filter mask. An hour would be considered an extended time frame. They tend to put an extra workload on the heart and respiratory system. It is also a good idea to store your mask in an airtight plastic bag. The filters tend to last longer if you do this.

Gloves

Different tasks require different type of gloves. There are a number of distributors of gloves. It is a good idea to find a good glove or safety rep who can supply you with gloves that will be effective with the chemicals you are using. I like the above-the-elbow length for cleaning. I favor the silver shield gloves for the really tough stuff like stripper.

Spray Suits

It is a good idea to protect as much of your skin as possible. Spray suits are inexpensive. They come with hoods or without, with feet or without them.

Chapter 8
MARKETING

Quick Tips for Getting Business

Hey, guys. It is now 2009. I have been a refinisher for eight years. I still like what I do. This chapter is a revision, an updated version of the original chapter I wrote in 2004. My marketing strategy has changed out of necessity over the past few years. I've picked up knowledge as I have rolled along.

The information presented in this book in the earlier chapters holds up well. Fundamentally, I wouldn't want to change any of it. After all, I wrote it when I was just getting started. If I were just getting started writing this book today I would perhaps gloss over too many elements. It is too easy to forget what you didn't know back then.

Anyway, back to marketing. The following are, in rank order, the best means I have for promoting my business.

The Internet

I see three significant ways to market your business. The internet, the internet, the internet. Seventy percent of my business comes from internet traffic. Granted, I am still only working by myself and have a limited amount of commercial business. For my business model, it is all about the internet.

You need a web-site. I don't mean to brag (okay maybe I do), but I get a lot of compliments on my web-site, www. evanstontubs.com. People tell me I seem credible and it's easy to follow. I really don't mind if any of my readers choose to borrow from it. I'll never see your site anyway.

If you are not a web designer, find someone who is a web designer to build your site. Preferably, this should be someone who can raise your ranking in the search engine and get traffic directed your way. If not, Google Adwords can bring traffic to you.

I have talked to other refinishers who do not utilize internet advertising, fully or at all. This is a huge, huge mistake. I no longer even choose to bother with print advertising. Two years ago I had one Yellow Book ad running to the tune of $170.00 a month. It pulled almost nothing. Forget Yellow Book, Yellow pages, yellow anything. Be particularly wary of Yellow Book or Yellow Pages promotional offerings. On that occasion, I took an ad at a greatly reduced rate with Yellow Pages. It turned out it was left over space they were trying to peddle. I found out the hard way these ads do not pull. Print ads just don't work for me. I have had particularly poor success with a Welcome Wagon sponsorship I took on in the last couple of years.

Of course, webmasters will tell you that they cannot always guarantee you a high ranking in the search engines. Any discussion involving search engine rankings is beyond the scope of my knowledge or this book. At the current time I do not have a top ten, first page, ranking in the search engines (Google, AOL, MSN). I rely solely on pay per click advertising.

When I started in this business, a good friend of mine initially worked on my web site and found ways to get me up there in the search engine rankings. Then, one day, about a year and half later, I lost my high search engine ranking overnight. My business tanked accordingly. My husband, who is a programmer, was able to help me get it back up there temporarily. But this proved to be an on-going challenge.

Google, the premier search engine, is prone to changing the rules. This is exactly what happened. Subsequently, I found myself having to do some reading on how search engines work.

I picked up a few pointers that can't hurt. Unfortunately, as I've stated, my search engine ranking isn't all that high these days. It definitely seems harder to raise my ranking than it did a few years ago.

Here are a couple of tips: 1) put the words "Bathtub Refinishing and Repair" on the top third of your home page in larger bold lettering. Put most of your descriptive key words in the same area. Know that if you try to repeat your key words too many times, it will actually work against you. Google does not look favorably upon this practice.

2) The actual purpose of the search engine is to guide the user in finding information. Unfortunately, Google (as a search engine anyway) is not in business to help you promote yours. This is why the rules for search engine ranking often favor government, educational and other informational web-sites. It is not a bad idea to offer an informational page with your site. An example might be a frequently asked questions page.

This leads me to my next topic: the use of Google Adwords. I have great success with them. Consequently, they get their own heading.

Google Adwords

What Google taketh away from me (by robbing me of my search engine ranking) Google has given back through Adwords. Adwords involve pay per click advertising. You can set your ad campaign in the region you are doing business.

When a potential customer uses the search engine to search for "bathtub refinishing" in the Chicago area, my Google Adwords pay per click ads appear. They show up off to the right or above the search engine listings, usually under "sponsored ads." I pay per time the potential customer clicks. Since it is a bidding system (a discussion that is beyond the scope of this book) the price per click can vary. I have paid between $.99 and $2.23 per click. Usually it floats around $1.50.

I can set up a daily budget. Normally, my daily budget is set at $8.00. Because the caller often books further down the road, I can't always tell how effective they are for me. However, anecdotally, I don't believe I am paying more than $20-25.00 per lead.

The nice thing about Google Adwords is this: If they aren't working for you (or working too well) you can shut them down or adjust your daily budget. Phone book ads are another story. Once the ink dries on the contract you are stuck with the ad. I have had my share of underachieving ads and know the frustration of having to pay for ineffective ads.

Perhaps you have heard that pay per click is ineffective. Actually, for this industry, it is ideal for several reasons. We are involved with small jobs. There is not a great deal of competition in any given market. The customer sees few ads. Most consumers regard choosing a tub refinisher as a fairly low stakes decision process, the fact that this may not be true notwithstanding. If your web-site stands out and you sound credible over the phone, you are likely to be hired.

Google has a free on-line tutorial. The web-sites involved are: adwords.google.com and www.google.com/adwords/learningcenter. I have found their tech support staff to be excellent. Now, naturally, you can hire someone to manage your campaign for you, but honestly, it's not necessary. Even a non-computer whiz like me became familiar by studying for a few hours over at two weeks time period. You can learn it.

Referral Business

I do get my share of referral business. Needless to say, it makes a pretty big difference. It would be a bit unfortunate if there were no way to garner repeat business. [Note: in 2008 about 30% of my business is referral business]. Honestly, however, my referral business will never sustain me. I am out there doing mostly small jobs. I have to keep the work coming in. For this reason I have to keep uncovering new opportunities. In short, referral business does not carry me.

Angie's List

This powerful list generates many leads. Angie's List gives me many referrals. Most major markets have an Angie's List office. Visit their web-site at Angieslist.com. The list was started by a woman, presumably named Angie who became fed up with less than professional contractors and subcontractors. She decided to generate a list of customer recommended names of remodelers, plumbers, electricians, you name it. These days a consumer can even hire a clown for his/her child's Christmas party off Angies List. The catch is, the homeowner or client must pay $60.00 a year for the list. It is a very good thing to be a vendor or service person listed on Angie's List.

I cheated a bit to get listed on Angie's List as a subcontractor, but I'd like to think it was legal. I simply approached a customer whom I know was satisfied with my work. I told her I would buy them a free subscription (membership) to Angie's List providing they would give me a favorable reference. I paid for memberships for two homeowners. This was enough to get the ball rolling. I started getting calls from other members of Angie's List, who in turn gave me a favorable reference. The momentum helped. I probably average a couple of calls a week off of Angie's list.

While I am on the subject, I will also tell you I personally have not had much luck with the type of referral lists that charge you per referral they generate for you. I've tried using them a couple of times. Many callers seemed to be price shopping. I don't have the cheapest prices and normally lose out. Also, sometimes the work was something I really didn't want to take. I was paying for those referrals. I could not make these services work.

One caveat, however. I don't think I would try to get myself on Angie's List until I had been in the business for a year or two. The customer must be very happy with your work or he/she might not be inclined to help you maintain a positive rating. Your work will be improving for the first couple of years. Don't get me wrong. You will still be getting paid for it. It is simply safe there is a learning curve to putting out very, very good work.

Marketing by Sharing Information

I may be unique in this regard, but I tend to share as much information as possible. I may even refer work to a competitor if it's something I don't want to handle. Sure, this may be costing me referral business but you'd be surprised. Sometimes a company will call me back again. I simply believe that doing the best you can for a customer will always come back to you in a good way.

The refinishing business is a unique one in that customers calling you often have other needs. They are looking for tilers, remodelers, or someone to remove an old bathtub. I know a number of contractors. I try to refer them work because they do the same for me. I actually do some on the job selling for them. It is very easy for me to ask customers what other types of work they need done. It is easy to do this in conjunction with my own work. I even have one friend who is a general contractor who lists "bathtub refinishing" in his advertising. He's never done a tub in his life, however he finds the listing gets him other business. You might suggest this tip to a contractor you know. Explain to the contractor that he can give the business to you. In the mean time, you both can benefit.

Magnetic Signs

Magnetic signs are an effective way to get business. In peak season (summer in Chicago) I get about one call a week directly off the signs on my S-10 pick-up truck. I have signs on the sides and one on the tailgate. Although I cannot substantiate this, I also feel I get business indirectly off my signs as well. Every year the numbers of calls I get increases. No doubt this has something to deal with brand familiarity, the fact that people keep seeing my truck around town. I know there is a reason Coca Cola likes to keep its name out there. I am often complimented on my signs. The artwork is flashy and lends credibility to my operation. If you work outside of my market feel free to steal my design. It is the one displayed on my web-site at www.evanstontubs.com. For more information simply e-mail me at andiscottb@mail.com.

Hometown Newspapers

I have tried advertising in a couple of local newspapers very little success. Of course, I have always heard that this needs to be done consistently before one can reap the benefits. This may be true. I am one who gave up early on this strategy. As I have indirectly stated, I simply don't have a lot of faith in any form of print advertising.

Cold Calls

Hey, any form of advertising works and I won't rule out cold calls. I sometimes call on property managers regarding tub and countertop work. Because I do repair work I stop at trailers on-site at new home developments. Cold calling may not be the most efficient or expedient way to drum up business but it can work. I did try it early on when I was trying to jump start my business. I called tilers and rehabbers and told them about my work. It met with some success.

Direct Mail

I have had some success with direct mail advertising. Remodelers will respond to them to a certain degree. I do have a small chip repair following I garnered from sending mailers to new home developers. I have not done them enough to generate any concrete statistics.

I have tried putting flyers on cars at places like Home Depot. This is also a fairly inefficient way to market your business. Seemingly, my return has been one call per 400 flyers. Not too good. Also, time consuming.

Home Improvement Stores

I have varying degrees of success with giving my cards to home improvement stores. Some are skittish about giving out names of contractors for fear they might be implicated if something goes wrong. The smaller hardware stores in my community have given me the most business. I would want to emphasize I haven't gotten a lot of business this way.

Other Advertising

Other forms of advertising include door hangers in neighborhoods where you have just completed work, large signs on the front lawn when you are working, tee-shirts and hats with your company name on them. Your supplier may even have a marketing department that supplies some of the items for you. Marketing opportunities are limited only by your imagination. I have not used any of the aforementioned methods mentioned in this paragraph.

This concludes my book. Feel free to stay in touch with me. My email address is: andiscott@gmail.com. As I have stated earlier, I believe it is only to my benefit to share what I learn.

I am putting this book on Amazon.com. If you choose to review it, be gentle. This is a niche industry. I have put a great deal of work into this manual, but I don't sell many copies. I assure you, if I did, I could afford to format it and package it quite differently. As it is, I am sure you will get your money's worth. I don't know where else this information can be obtained. Best of luck.

MATERIALS AND SUPPLY LIST

HVLP GUN
TURBINE
EXHAUST SYSTEM
DROP CLOTHES
CLEANING SUPPLIES
WET/DRY SANDPAPER, 80-100 GRIT FOR MOST PREP WORK, 220 FOR FINER NEEDS, 400-600 FOR SANDING ROUGHNESS LATER
1500-2000 SANDPAPER (FOR BUFFING OUT SMALL SCRATCHES ON ACRYLIC SURFACES. ALSO USE FINESSE).
MASKING TAPE, GENERAL PURPOSE. FREE RELEASE FOR DELICATE PAINT AND WALLPAPER
3M BLUE TAPE FOR MASKING DRAIN
BINS FOR STORING COATINGS
TOOL BOX
RAZOR BLADES WITH SAFETY EDGE
BONDO OR POLYESTER BODY FILLER
PUTTY FOR SMOOTHING HAIRLINE SCRATCHES. TWO TO TRY: 3M ACRYLIC RED GLAZING PUTTY OR 3M MARINE PUTTY #05962.
SOLVENT OR OVERSPRAY AND GUN CLEANER
CUPS FOR MEASURING COATINGS
PAINT STIR STICKS
GLOVES, LATEX FOR MIXING PAINT, ELBOW LENGTH FOR CLEANERS, ETCH (HYDRACHLORIC ACID) RESISTANT GLOVES
GREEN PAINTER'S PAPER (WILL NOT BLEED-THROUGH)

SCOTCH BRITE PADS

PAPER TOWEL (CHEAPER THE BETTER, LEAVES LESS RESIDUE)

GARBAGE BAGS

ELECTRIC SANDER EITHER ORBITAL OR VIBRATING. A COR-NER CAT OR MOUSE SANDER IS ALSO USEFUL IF YOU NEED TO HIT THE EDGES.

PLASTIC SPREADERS FROM AN AUTO PAINT STORE FOR FILL-ING WIDE CHIPS

SMALL FUNNELS WITH TUBING FOR JOBS WHERE FAUCET LEAKS. WILL ROUTE WATER TO DRAIN OR OVERFLOW

INEXPENSIVE SHOP VACUUM (UNDER $30.00 AT K-MART)

FINESSE POLISH FROM AUTO PAINT STORE FOR POLISHING TUB

MSDN SHEETS SHOULD BE CARRIED IN YOUR VEHICLE, IN CASE YOU ARE STOPPED BY THE POLICE

STRIPPER

FULL COMPLEMENT OF SCREWDRIVERS, INCLUDING VERY SMALL ONES

OPTIONAL: TRIM KITS AND CONSUMER CLEANERS

ALSO: IN CASE YOU RUN INTO A CUSTOMER WHO DOESN'T UNDERSTAND YOU ARE NOT A HANDY:

UTILITY KNIFE

PRY BAR

(THE LATTER STEMS FROM AN INCIDENT WHERE THE CUSTOM-ER WANTED SHOWER DOORS PERMANENTLY REMOVED AND THOUGHT IT WAS INCLUDED IN MY PRICE. I CHRARGED FOR THIS, BUT YOU HAVE TO HAVE THE TOOLS).

MILK CRATES WORK WELL FOR CONSOLIDATING CONTAIN-ERS FOR COATINGS.

RESOURCE GUIDE

Axis Products
858-536-7960
Fresh Air Respirator and HVLP Paint Sprayer Combination System

C J SPRAY
370 Airport Road
South St. Paul, MN 55075
Phone: 651-455-1213
Graco HVLP turbine spray equipment

Grainger
1-888-361-8649
carpet fan exhaust system

Integrity Coatings
2797 Irving Blvd
Dallas, TX 75207
800-773-7336 or 214-631-8717
Complete supply house for refinishing and training

Kleen-Strip Aircraft Remover, water soluble
Aircraft stripper available at Pep Boys auto supply store

Multitech Products
41519 Cherry Street
Murrieta, CA 92562
1-800-218-2066
www.multitechproducts.com

Complete repair systems for appliances, bathtubs, sinks, tile and surrounds

North American Polymer Company Ltd
4426 N. Ravenswood
Chicago, IL 60640-5803
773-506-8881
Complete supply house for refinishing and training

Paasche Airbrush Co.
7440 W. Lawrence
Harwood Heights, IL 60706
708-867-9191
Airbrush guns and accessories

Saf-T-Gard International
205 Huehl
Northbrook, IL 60062
847-291-1600
Safety Equipment

Spraytech
1770 Fernbrook Lane
Minneapolis, MN 55447
612-553-7000
Wagner HVLP equipment

Watco Manufacturing Company
1220 South Powell Road
Independence, MO 64057-2724
816-796-3900
Trim kits

TRAINING PROGRAMS

North American Polymer Company (Napco)
Skokie, IL (suburban Chicago)
Duration: 2-3 days or a week
Web-site: www.napcoltd.com
Phone: 800-888-1081
Trainer: Mike Ripp

Integrity Coatings
Dallas, TX
Duration: 2 and a half days
Web-site: www.integritrycoatings.com
Phone: 800-773-7336 or 214-631-8717
Trainer: Phil Anderson

Jim Sharp, Sharp Porcelain
Grapevine, TX (Dallas area)
Duration: 1-2 weeks
Web-site: www.sharpporcelain.com
Phone: 817-481-3670 or 817-421-0381
Trainer/business owner/operator: Jim Sharp

www.ingramcontent.com/pod-product-compliance
Lightning Source LLC
Chambersburg PA
CBHW061838220326
41599CB00027B/5332